Perfect Reflection

Destany Stevens

Published by Wild Hearts Write Differently™
Maine, USA

ISBN: 979-8-9961774-0-0
ISBN: 979-8-9961774-1-7

Cover art by aeriiuna
Interior art by Destany Stevens
Interior formatting by Destany Stevens

Content Note:

This collection was written during a period of recognizing and seeking treatment for a mood disorder. The poems trace cycles of perception, dissociation, clarity, and reflection that accompanied that discovery. These pieces reflect moments of noticing, survival, and learning to advocate for oneself.

These poems are not meant to provide answers, but to document moments of awareness and the process of learning to advocate for oneself.

Reader Advisory:

Some poems in this collection contain references to:

- Depression
- Intrusive thoughts and suicidal ideation
- Self-harm imagery
- Sexual assault
- Substance use
- Trauma and memory
- Dissociation and mental health struggles

Readers are encouraged to engage with the collection at their own pace and with care.

Table of Contents

—

The turn is up here
a flicker
Is it considered suicide?
i’m sorry
Ajar

Perfect Reflection

The floor is cold and slick beneath me—
shallow breaths, eyes swollen shut.
Chocking up, thrashing;
my body chooses for me.

Shoulders trembling.
Breathe in.
Breathe out.

In—

The air begins to seep from my lungs.
Dragging the panic away.

Eyes blured.
Chesk tightens,
around,
each breath.

A sob snags
splintering into something
indescribable.

My breath stutters
laughter tears from my chest.
Uneven bursts begin to echo,
breathless and brittle.

Too much.

A crumpled face,
throat hoarse,
burning,

I begin to curl into myself;

hands lost.

My scalp itches—
like little bugs
skittering beneath my skin.

I unravel, rooting into place.

A sniffle.
A wipe of her cheek.

Pushing myself upright,
legs trembling below.

I slip as if I am wearing
skates on freshly cleaned ice.

Heart pounding,
the room begins to tilt.
I rise to full height.

A lift of my chin—
not in defiance,
but in certainty.

The mirror catches me standing.

She's staring at me.
She looks—

She looks exhausted.

Heavy-lidded,
bags so deep
you can't find the bottom.

Weight lifting.
Chest heaving.

A sharp breath.
Standing.

Watching.

I begin to copy her—wash my face.

Scrub, lather, repeat.

Hands shaking,
face masked.

Like porcelain,
her face, perfect and unfractured.

She blots her swollen lips.
Color deepens,
she looks at me.

Her shoulders are resting.
Her posture

asking for no defense.

Uncounted.
Unafraid—

She stands with ease,
as if tiles are holding her in place.

Her expression holds no fear.

Composure falters.
A creack
I almost miss it.

She breathes.

Releasing her soul
to the air.
She swallows it whole.

Fighting for breath.

Like a fish on a hook.
She reels herself in.

Eyes lock.

Face flushed and numb.

I follow suit, eyes closed.
Tightening till we see spots.
Shaking my hands out.

We sneak a peek,
we smile.
It's contagious,
we can't help but gleam.

Her eyes dart to the counter.

My favorite perfume...

I take a deep inhale,
I love this scent.
Blackcurrant and musk
I spritz myself.

not once.
Twice—

Smiling.
Eyes hollow.

Lying still.
Almost asleep.

Her face;
a rigid porcelain doll.

painted to perfection,

Unblinking.

Living Dead Mom

The alarm goes off.
"up, mama, up."
A groan of displeasure.

Light creeps in.
The dog snorts, and I sigh.

I plaster a smile
"Up, mama, up."
"Come snuggle."

"mommy"
Shoulders shook.

I picked the pacifier up off the floor.

Every step,
every moment
feels heavy.

I put the toys away.

Please don't pull my hair.

I literally.
Just said.

Please.

Don't.

Pull.
Mama's hair.

Fucking,
Stop—

Take another dose.

Living dead mom.

Embrace

His hand is warm,
like his embrace.

It wraps me
in a net
of comfort.

Callosed hands,
scent of sweat
mixed with Old Spice.

So calm,
so peaceful.

All I need
is

his wam

          embrace...

a good day

Sometimes all you need
is good company,
a good book,

and a long drive.

Well, that,
a few stiff drinks
and a visit to the casino.

Soft looks,
whispered plans.

a small break
followed by a few
fast-acting tablets.

For me, it is
a mirage,
as if I were in a trance.

it's all we need.

click, loop, echo

Clickity Clickity click.
Clickity click.
Click.
Click.
Click.

Click.

Click—

Click—

The echo of Teams notifications
ding in my dreams.

Nostrils flare; darting eyes.
Rhythmic thumping.

Another meeting.
Brain stutter.

Tap, tap, tap,
tap, tap, tap

Echo.
Echo.

Another notification.

"Can we chat for a sec?"

Dread…

Tap, tap, tap,
tap, tap, tap

"Oh, I just wanted to ask
a quick question."

Shrill, internal screams.
Banshee cries.

Are you fucking kidding me?
Stop—

cacophony

I am a blank space
with blurred vision.

I close my eyes,
my shoulders slump.

Strings attached.
Head bobs.

Like a marionette

Deep, jerky inhale.
Ragdoll shoulders.

A shuddered exhale.

Gaze shrinking.
Rounding,
narrow and rigid.

I have a gag reflex like
pressure on

hairline fractures in glass

Blurry pupils.
Head tilted.

Ears ringing
at the sounds around me.

Clenched jaw

air pulling.

Release—

Gagging, gasping for breath.

Ice snaps and flows.
Spine frozen, static.

Shards crash
with a silent shutter.

Body convulsing
shivering.

Wrinkled nose.
Pinched lips.

Shoulders stiffen
rise—
and
fall—

of my chest.

Exhausted gaze.

Warmth begins to seep in.
Eyes flutter.

conscious…
again.

Descent

Most Days

Most days, she is like
a ghost within
the house's walls.

Warmth leached from her skin,
her heart
and soul.

Solid yet fractured

like the world around her—

She is in need,

I need help,
I am afraid of
what I might do.

Ray—

of hope,
a foreign feeling.

Its warmth
is like a stranger

she staggers
she falls
picked back up.
But pieces remain.

Do better?

Do better.

Do better?
I'm trying.

To get my head on straight.

Do not give in to the thoughts.

My thoughts are macabre

and my brain?

Don't even get me started.
One thing leads to another
and I'm in a rabbit hole
of emotions

crying on the kitchen floor.

That one's usually told as a joke

but it's true.

It's where I spend most of my breaks

these days.

I am depressed.

I don't think it's abnormal,
but who am I to know?

I am extremely high.
It seems like that's most of the time.

I like to think of it as self-medicating.
Others might see it as substance abuse.

It totally is.

But I am depressed.

I looked at my daughter this morning
and faded out of existence.

I dissociated for a moment,
and it was one of the only times

I had

pure, unadulterated
silence

all day.

I am exhausted
and hungry.

I have the munchies
I am depressed.

Depressed

My protein bar feels like a lump
making its way down,
like sandpaper.

My head feels like a brick
against my shoulder.

Did I get a kiss?
I am…

depressed.

Blank

My husband just came over
and handed me a protein bar.

I think he gave me a kiss.

My lips feel buzzed
and chilled,
as if the warmth

that might have been there
Is now absent.

It's like looking out from the inside.

I missed the highlight reel.

My veins are filled with lead.

Dragging my eyelids,
almost sealed shut.

I just know it was silent
Because of nothing processed.

I don't know
what I saw
or heard.

My brain is blank,
like ice in a thaw.

I am still.

Numb,
lips still buzzing.

I am high as could be,
and I think I'm still drinking my…

tea?

I miss the clouds.

My brain won't stop reeling.
My stomach hurts.

I am depressed.

This long drive

with you

it is made of soft
fairytales

music and sunsets
resting at the top
of a hill

falling,

falling,

down–

the music rings
through my brain

every crease, every fold,
entranced by the sound.

“worst turn ever created.”
it feels like I’m fading

in and out

I wish we could
always go for
long drives.

Oscillation

Manic

Up, down, left, right.

Which way do I go?

Decide—

You make me so happy.
Blissfully ignorant

waiting for the other
shoe to drop

I love you,
you make me happy.
I crave you.

I need you—

you smell
disgusting.

But you smell

amazing.

You are intoxicating.

Please don't touch me.

I can't stand the smell of your breath—

I love you.
You smell like maple syrup.
So sweet, so innocent.

I adore you.

Blonde hair, cherub cheeks
green eyes, pale skin.

Demon,
satan's mistress.

Seraph,
my favorite

you make me
a demon.

I would burn it all down.

I will burn it all down for you.
Just ask.

Please.

Anything you want,
it's yours.

I love you—

Please don't touch me.
Don't come near me

I don't hate you
But—

I can't be near you
My brain hurts

Don't.

Don't…
Touch me.

Don't...
Talk to me

Leave.

Me.

alone—

Sunset mountains

Sunset mountains

filled with shadows

made up of silhouettes.

The devil is
not welcome today

the sky is free of

cloudy

behaviors and moods

hand in hand,
warmth rests

in my lap

feeling higher
in this

dusky

evening

I am

addicted.

To this feeling,

to you,
to these

Sunset mountains.

Clarity

Ready!
Set!
Go!

Her shouts
ringing in the air.

Arms out.
Head tipped back
.
Round
and
around.

Warm giggles

spun across the living room

she has ice cream
I have hot chocolate.

She has a sweater
I have pounds of blankets.

I am shivering.
She is sweating.

"Where'd paci go?"

You just said a full sentence…

She

is so big.

So grown.

Please stay.

clean

The faucet's hiss rings in my ears.
The hot mist rises, fogging the glass.

My hand wipes across
the misted surface.

Shivering.
Frigid glass beneath,
my fingertips.
A jolt to the system.

I see my reflection.
My hair stringy and tangled.

Eyes, lips,
dark and puffy.

Tugging.
Pulling.
Brushing.

I'm a mangled mess.

Towel in hand,
face exfoliated,
stripped and bare.

Hands loosening,
pressure lingering.

Needy hands.
A phantom towel
making its way across my face.

Bursts of adrenaline.

Shell-shocked.
Breath hitching,
trapped,

Skin left tight.

raw—

scratch

Nails.
They are jagged and bumpy.

Making their way
across my skin.

Neck,
shoulders,
back,

and face—

My torso suddenly strained
shoulders pulling tight.

Toes taut,
stretched and erect.

a strained breath
wheezes its way through.

It is
instant relief.

lilt

Tired and
fatigued.

It seeps into her bones.
and her soul.

The world heavy,
binding,
forcing

her eyes shut.
The ticking of a clock.

It chimes,
12 o'clock—

the room
it swivels and pulls.

mismatched socks,

a small fissure
slowly unraveling.

How—
how did I get here?

I am so—
tired.

I feel lost
and muddled.

Rythmically swaying
with leaden feet,
dragging me towards

the bed.

My throat aches.
breath no longer escapes.

I am as dry as the Sahara.

It's dark.

I am a broken dam.

fragility

She is...
Crystalline and glacial.

Her memories
reduced to shadowy tendrils

Their actions
are not her reflection.

Dismantled razor blades,
red streams,
and raw emotion.

Slices disguised
like paper cuts.

Scars are left,
reminiscent of the past.

Alluring mistakes
masked in splendor.

Each slice
more provocative
then the next.

She is left
completely devoid—

like te walk of shame

Volatile and erratic.
Steeling herself for the inevitable.

Still breathing, still scared.

Fear of breaking down
what is already shattered.

She is delicately mosaicked,

a work of art.

a standstill

My favorite show plays in the background.
Abusers, rapists, and murderers.

Not sure why,
but these moments seem
calm,
serene.

Not overstimulating.

Down the hall, I hear
it—
up and down.
up and down.

Giggles erupting.

"Is Mee-maw teaching you
to play with the
exercise bands?"

Her giggles intensify.
My heart is a puddle.

My thoughts?
A standstill.

Finally...

Like Her Mother

Clear mind,
haunted soul.

Constantly afraid of
where I might go.

Watching her grow,
day by day.

Longer hair,
bright green eyes,
cheeky girl,

smart-mouth
like her mother.

Lashing out
like her mother.

Fear of
cycling,
syncing.

Wide eyes and shock,
the recollection of self.

She is me
and I am her.

We are the same,
please turn out differently.

Please don't be like Mama..

I hope you are
safe,
healthy,
and bright.

Your innocence intanct,
mine in the wind.

Precious girl,
you deserve more.

Mourning the girl
who is now lost.

You are still whole
alive,

I am
a shell
a husk

I wish you more.

thin

Soft skin, button nose.
Flused lips, stiffened spine.

My twin,
my life,
my reflection.

Leaping through time.

disapearing like stars at daylight

you are
my joy,
my pride,.
You are my exhaustion.

My gaze meets your profile.

So young, so big.

Polar spectrums.
Mirror image.

We are a pair.
Matched at conception.

You grow brighter.

In the mirror,

I fade.

Reckoning

i remember

i remember the first...
time,

when i first experienced
self-harm and hate.

i remember the two
fighting over me

it's my turn to mary her!
no, she's my wife.
but it's my turn with her!

No...
she's mine.

five-year difference
isn't such a difference.

covered in soft light
and blankets

face lilting downward
warm breath
shaky limbs

shadows.
silence.
movement to the right

like someting
skulking in the night.

fingers tight
soft breaths

red-faced and ashamed

"oh look, i got her pocketknife."
"give that back! it's my birthday gift."

core memory

what?
what did you just fucking say?

A snapshot
frozen in time.

Brooding gase and
nostrils flaired.

Slowly standing.

The force of him
pushes the chair away.

kinetic energy
doing what it does best.

Shoulders swaying,
heavy strides.

A table flips
and a baby cries.

Like a gorilla
his head is lowered
with every stride.

He closes the distance.

Without knowing

I follow,
watching,
waiting,

ready to pounce
at the moment of danger.

"Get the hell out of there."

Snapping quickly,
I turn in stride

serpentine
around the room
and for the door.

Warm, sticky air
gasping for breath.

"shit, I forgot the baby bag."
"you can't go back in there."
"I have to. stay here."

Do

Not

Move.

Door slams.
Car starts.

Gravel turns
beneath the wheels.

escape

It’s been a few days.
We need to talk
about when you’re

going to return.

Breathless exhale.

I’m
not.

Unofficially

Have you ever attempted suicide?

Unofficially.

Eyebrow raised.
Questions circling in her gaze.

when you are young and dumb
you don't know much
about anatomy.

so when you play
with a blade
and that itchy itch

when the blood runs deep
it just
doesn't seem to stop...

the fog fills you with
evanescence.

"oh fuck."

Pause.

Isn’t it funny
how staring out a window
at the kitchen sink
can feel

like snowlfakes

falling

to the ground
like specks of glitter

floating

all

around

like a—

as well as can be

I feel well.
As well as can be,
Zoloft and Lexapro.

I feel dead inside,
static—

a lump of wet ash.

I am well,
as well as can be,

I lock myself in the bathroom,
a moment of peace.

I am not quite right.

Mama. Okay?
—
Okay, mama?

Sitting on the kitchen floor.
It's my lunch hour.

Some days,
I weep for the girl
I could've been.

Some days

Some days,
I am not a girl
I am a women,

alone on the floor
under her bookshelf.

The sun is shining bright.
Blinds are drawn.

The salt runs down my face.
The clock chimes
again and again,

I am unimportant—

Some days,
I want to succumb.
To die—

Some days
I'm numb.

Subdued

Face painted
like porcelain.

She protects herself
with a thin shell.

She has endured.

More tragedy than comedy.
More comedy then tragedy.

Stuck and numb,
waiting to be unearthed.

I sleep in a shallow grave,
bathed in daisies.

Most wear rose-colored glasses.
Mine are as dim
and my mind as stable
as loose gravel.

rickety stick

Constantly stuck.

Between
the two—
never with either.

Off-kilter.

I am holding
it all
up—

I am
a rickety stick

holding a life
on
its
edge.

Unspoken

I hear his
slurred words
and emptry promises.

I see little girls
he mentions dainty skirts.

Novocains on Sunday.

Fake pleasantries
and rising delusions.

Slipped comments

and denial.

The lies, the fear,

circling the drain,
finding the bottom
of the bottle—

I remind myself

don't allow your friends inside.

Keep them safe
and to the side.

Swaying steps,
ignorance is bliss.

Doubt—

Mistrust while astray.
A veiled imposter,

sick and in pain.
Excuses made in vain.

—

run,
pause.
stop all motion.

stillness.
silence,
a blanket of snow.

swollowed by the void.
vantablack.

no light.
no sparkle.

just

DARK—

Emergence

The turn is up here

Into the light?

Oh yes,
wonderfully so.

Wrinkled side looks,
a sigh of laughter

resting back.

The sunset view

in this

long drive

home.

a flicker

sparking
heat
permeates

in the
clouds

dark circles

recognizable
scars

a silver
lining

warmth
glistens

raindrop
trails

exhaustion
sleep
rest;

Is it considered suicide?

I passed a church today and thought—if I go in, can they tell me why I shouldn't kill myself?

Do you ever have thoughts about harming yourself or others?

Never others, just myself…it's always

myself—

I saw a big red truck driving toward me. It made me think—what would happen if I drove straight into it?

Is that considered a suicidal thought or intent to harm? If I plan to hurt myself, but it takes someone with me, is it plotting?

I don't usually think about killing myself so much as I think about being dead.

Would you say you have chronic suicidal ideation?

Probably. But I'm not sure now.

Thinking about that question more and more. I wonder—is it considered suicide if you think of the ways you could die rather than inflicting it? If I do think of suicide, it's never a gun. It's not romantic enough.

Most days, I'm either high up in the sky or lower than dirt. I am numb and often succumb to the smaller sins.

Slitting my throat or my wrists so that the bloodletting can release my sorrows, my pain?

What pain?

My brain is often lost, and I can't tell if I am suicidal or obsessed with the macabre.
While driving, I count the times I think about dying.

Seven.
On my drive home.

As for the drive-in, I have no idea. The thought of counting didn't occur to me until I recapped the conversation with my therapist in my mind, which had gotten lost in transit. I saw the bridge by my house, and the intrusive thought of just continuing—driving up and over the edge—came to me.

Is that considered suicide or a lapse in thought?

If I don't think about killing myself so much as I think about being dead, is it still considered suicide?

I'm sorry

I'm sorry,

I think I'm having a bad day.

I'm sorry—
I think I spaced out.

I'm sorry,
I don't know what time it is.

I'm sorry,
I didn't know you were mad.

I'm sorry,
I'm feeling kind of tired.

I'm sorry—
I didn't realize I said that.

I'm sorry,
I spaced out again.

I'm sorry…
I made you upset.

I'm sorry,
I think I did really well today.

I'm sorry,
I didn't mean to bother you.

I’m sorry,
I’m really proud of myself.

I’m sorry,
I think I’m going to be sick.

Sorry,
I’m not sure why I keep saying it.

But—

I am.

Ajar

Light through the cracks
of brain fog—
lost moments,
missing emotions.

The bathroom door was left ajar.
I am a shattered mess,

like the remnants of an exploding
light bulb.

Light pools on the floor.
She brings me back.

Are you ready to wake up, baby?
It's time to get up.

She rolls,
stifles a giggle.
She smiles.

She is light.

She…
is my reality.

She is my home.
We are safe.

Acknowledgements

To my partner in crime and the love of my life, Ray, thank you for supporting me through all the late nights, long days, and emotional ups and downs. Your love and patience carried me through this process more than you know.

To Justin, my best friend and anchor in more ways than one, thank you for keeping me grounded when I overthink and for always reminding me to stay present and mindful.

To my mom, thank you for standing beside me through every high and low and for always being a source of honesty, encouragement, and unwavering love.

To Mariah, thank you for putting up with my indecisiveness and for curating the perfect art for Perfect Reflection. Thank you for being such a bright source of light in my life.

Follow Online

Instagram: @destanybstevens
TikTok: @destanybstevens
Facebook: Destany Stevens, Author
Linkedin: @Destany Stevens

Reviews Matter

If you enjoyed this collection, please consider leaving a review on Amazon, Goodreads, or your favorite bookseller platform. Reviews help readers discover new books and support independent authors.

Thank you for being part of this journey.
— Destany Stevens

www.ingramcontent.com/pod-product-compliance
Lightning Source LLC
LaVergne TN
LVHW090332210926
848480LV00004B/1387